Logical Financially Fundamentals

Jacob Blankenship

Table of Contents

Preamble

In this book there are ideas and strategies that the writer will not assume any responsibility for. Practice these strategies and ideas at your own choice, but by choosing to do so you agree that the author is not responsible for any loss of money or for any gain in money.

As you read through this book realize this is to educate, and give ideas on how to better handle finances, many of the ideas have been tested and tried, and verified working, but this also depends on the mindset of the person doing the strategy, and the results will vary from person to person.

I wish everyone reading this luck in there journey, wealth in their life, and peace in all their dealings. May your mind continue to expand in knowledge and your life be well while you are on this realm.

I have studied fiances on my own for over three years, learning and trying many different approaches. I have bought many books, researched many articles, and before writing in this book, I have attempted everyone of them. I have even tried those make money quick schemes or programs, I advise avoiding every single one of them, learn from my annoyance at them.

In the end finances take education, hard work, budgets, risk, and luck. A magic bullet to become rich does not exist, but with effort and work you can still make it there.

Chapter 1

The Basics

Welcome to the basics. This chapter may end up being very boring for many people, however it is essential that the basics are mastered. This is the point where a sound and solid foundation will be built up and hold the empire you build up.

I personally like to think of finances as a high score and a game really. I asked another person I recently taught about finances if that is how they see it, the answer was an affirmative.

So in order to explain the basics, we will have to go to a time before the personal finance was removed out of school, and common core math was attempted to be introduced. I am not going to trick you, finances are pure math, and pure strategy. If you do not like math, that is okay, you can use tools such as calculators and spreadsheet formulas and I will show you how. Just don't give up and focus on building the foundation.

If you can imagine a time before spreadsheet programs and online bank accounts, people had to personally go to the banks in order to make deposits, and to make withdraws. They put every purchase in something called a check registrar. A time before ATM, check cards, and credit cards were common place, people wrote checks, and put balanced the check book. Below is an empty check registrar.

AD - Automatic Deposit • AP - Automatic Payment • ATM - Cash Withdrawal • DC - Debit Card • FT - Funds Transfer • SC - Service Charge • TD - Tax Deductible

NUMBER OR CODE	DATE	TRANSACTION DESCRIPTION	PAYMENT, FEE, WITHDRAWAL (-)	✓	DEPOSIT, CREDIT (+)	$	BALANCE

This is how finances were tracked back in the day, and actually technology and online, has really allowed people to forego true book keeping skills using such proven methods. It is easy to spend if you do not have to take the time to write a check and log it into the registrar. Just zip that card and go.

While technology is not a bad thing, it comes with that drawback, but it also has some perks for those that watch their money carefully. I mention the antiquated way because one must understand where some of the basic concepts came from. Concepts like balancing and budgeting come from the antiquated style of finances. It is not so much antiquated as it is rarely used now.

So let's go into the basics starting from knowledge you will know before a job. The core information of finances and we will see if I can change your mind about some of the terms, ideology, and concepts along the way.

In the finance world we have terminology, so let's break into that each time we have a new idea. This book will define, then tell you why it is important, and then make a seemingly off in left field analogy about it, or a joke.

Money – Noun - a current medium of exchange in the form of coins and banknotes; coins and banknotes collectively.

Basically the green stuff here in the United States, plus the coins. Actually for those being technical the green paper money in the states are actually promissory notes by the United States government. The saying goes, "Money makes the world go around".

Bank - Noun - a financial establishment that invests money deposited by customers, pays it out when required, makes loans at interest, and exchanges currency.

This is important to know about, because most things will travel through banks at some point of time. The piggy bank of the adult world. The difference is it gives you dividends that a oink piggy bank will not.

Deposit – Verb - a sum of money placed or kept in a bank account, usually to gain interest.

These items are important because this is the flow of money into an account, it is what builds up.

Withdraw – Verb - take (money) out of an account.

We want to avoid these at this time, until later, build up then when you take it will not be a big deal. Most people are murdered by these due to lack of self control.

Dividend - a sum of money paid regularly (typically quarterly) by a company to its shareholders out of its profits (or reserves).

While not all that high in the banks, a dividend is actual money given to you for the banks to hold (or use) your money.

With these three basic terms we now have what we need for the twelve year old to start banking. If your have an income of money, for allowances, or for holidays, you can open a savings account and start building up. Plus you actually already have the basic knowledge of how to manage a check registrar without even knowing it. General math will be your companion here.

You get your parents to go with you to the bank, and open an account. Try to do the talking yourself if you can. Put your name in their book and when the associate starts talking and helping you open the account, ask any questions you have, and do the talking. This will start a relationship with a customer instead of a kid. It will also allow you to network in the financial industry pretty quick.

Say you start off with a deposit of $100.00 into your savings account. So the registrar would read across.

Date: Name – Memo – Withdraw – Deposit – Total

12/25/2001 Deposit – Start account   +100.00   +100.00

We use plus and +-x to make it simple. All your doing is adding and subtracting really. So it you were to make a withdraw of 50.00 it would look like this from that starting point on the next line.

12/26/2001 Withdraw for x toy   +-50.00   +-50.00

                                                 +50.00

Basically your doing this in simple terms.

                    100.00

-50.00

50.00

That is essentially all your doing each time you deposit (add money) or withdraw (remove money). Just add the next line and do your math. Double check the math, or use a calculator to double check the work. It is better to be absolutely sure of the remaining balance so you do not withdraw more than what is in the account. This is important to know especially later on once we break out of the basics.

Now I want to get to the dirty part of finances, personal and business both do budgets. Through talking with people, when you mention that word they cringe or flat out hate it. Personally, a budget is not what limits your money, but the item that keeps you honest with your money, and plans for the financial future. Most people see it as an item of out going money, instead of what money they can keep, afford, or invest.

Budget – noun - an estimate of income and expenditure for a set period of time

The very essence of a budgeting is your dedication to control the financial future you. Without a budget, it is easy to over spend. You get behind and then you play catch up and sometimes, some people are unable to catch up, due to their lack of budgeting. If your thinking about buying a home, renting an apartment, a car, a kid, and so on, then a budget should be the first place to start in order to find your comfortable range of extra cash, because it will not be extra once you start calculating the extra out going cash or expenditure as some call it.

If you calculated that you do not have enough buy the house that would cost $600.00 a month on the mortgage, but you realize you can afford a $400.00 payment, then you know your current choices. Rent or own, owning a house has extra costs, like yard equipment, repairs, etc. So do not forget to calculate that in as well.

A statement needs to be made outside the realm of finances, but still has a grip in the finance world. When you look at finances don't stop there, be educated in all areas that has a hand in finances, like buying a house, having a kid, buying a car, even general or scholarly items has a grip in finances. Do not limit your mind with a single path or limit the mind's learning. Learn any and all things.

When it comes to decent parenting in the financial world, having a child present as you pay bills, or do the household budget helps them understand later how to start with a financial stronghold. Parents should welcome the children at a certain age (probably a year before they start to work), into the household budgeting sessions.

Budget – Noun – A plan created for a household or personal finance for future income.

Think of a budget as the general plan, the framework or floor plan of the finances. Now along the way you can make adjustments, add that extra room or shrink the house because it is not needed. It is more flexible than one thinks. Most people dislike it because they think it is an inflexible tool, however it is there to show you how much room you have, or how much you can create, but never to fully limit you.

If anything a budget will show you how much money you can save up a month, roughly, and where you can start putting money. A budget shows me if I can free up resources, or if I have resources to use. If I spend for example, $200.00 for cable and Internet, but realize I rarely watch T.V outside of the Internet, then why do I need to pay that much. I can reclaim some of that money by downgrading my package.

So how does one do a budget, what is involved in a budget. What parts are included in budgets and why? Well first let me do some quick definitions here. Income is the money coming to you in forms of pay checks, allowances, etc. Now if we put that car in reverse we have debt, the money leaving your account (or hands) to pay off a bill, or a loan.

So essentially the budget will have your income, and your debts. You can break it apart anyway you want, but I like separating information for ease of manipulation. In this case I am going to have a gentlemen named John who works as a cashier for minimum wage. John is just a teenager, and lives at home. Since he is still in school his mother and father does not at this time charge rent like any good parent that cares about the financial future of their kid would.

Now John works in Florida with 40 hour work weeks and the Florida minimum wage is $8.47. So using math I can say before taxes he get 40*8.47*4 for a month. So let's break down his bills. He bought a phone online for $200.00 unlocked and his cell bill is $40.00 a month.

We will also say he uses the parents car, and he is a rider on his parents insurance which charges $60.00 / month for him. John is no bum, and cares about his parents financial freedom so he pays his share. His fuel that he puts in the car is about $20.00 / week. Essentially that is his bills, I can not imagine anything else that a teen would purchase that is really necessary.

		The case of John in high school			
Gross	1355.2				
Net	1251.54				
Bills:					
Phone	-40				
Car Insurance	-60				
Fuel	-80				
Total:	-180				
Net Total:	1071.54				

So let me explain the formula's because it really helps. The gross income is what your employer pays before taxes, and the net is what you get after. It is easy to remember due to fishing terms, if you net something you get it, but all fish are gross.

So let's do a quick quiz, did this budget limit John? If you still think yes, lets do this. For 8 months John saves what is left. He now has $8,572.32 in savings. With another month John could purchase the following car.

Used 2001 Chevrolet Camaro Z28 Coupe $8,995

137,420 miles
White · 17 City / 26 Highway · 2 wheel drive - rear · 8-Cylinder

Network Transportation Inc (NTI) (7.7 mi. away)   Get AutoCheck Vehicle History
1 (888) 996-2579 | Confirm Availability

Straight out, no monthly payment. Now he will have a higher monthly premium, but it is not like he couldn't afford it. So let's say he does this. His savings goes back to $0.00 and his insurance rises to say $120 / month. Time to adjust budget for senior year, by this time most people would have received a raise but let's just stick with the numbers we have.

Gross	1355.2
Net	1251.54
Bills:	
Phone	-40
Car Insurance	-120
Fuel	-80
Total:	-240
Net Total:	1011.54

Within the first month he saved for most if not all the graduation costs of high school and his parents being as good as they are will pay half. Not only that he has saved a but load. Say more closer to $7,000.00 roughly after costs from school.

If John was happy where he was and did not want to go to college or further his career. He could perform the following:

The case of John in high school

Gross	1355.2		
Net	1251.54		
Bills:			Remember John has no car payment. After a 12 month lease he has a good chunk of change for a down payment of a home.
Rent	-400		
Phone	-40		
Car Insurance	-120		
Fuel	-80		
Electric/Water	-70		
Renter's Ins.	12		
Food / Stuff	200		
Total:	-498		
Net Total:	753.54		
	After 12 month lease:		
	9042.48		

Starting to see how a budget gives freedom to finances yet? John does, and he met a nice girl that enjoys his Z28 very much, actually she loves him and they enjoy each other. So time to modify again, as they are moving in together.

Now you add the income she would bring in. Say she too works as a cashier, and makes minimum wage. John being the responsible financial person he is, sits her down and says, if we are going to make it, we need to spend time with each other, and one way to do that is our monthly budget.

The case of John adult with girlfriend							
Gross	1355.2						
Net Household	2503.08	Single	1251.54				
Bills:			John's girlfriend went another route and has a car payment. It is expected that the costs go up,				
Rent	-400		so the safe bet is to double most things except for rent. They plan to get married after a year				
Phone	-80		living together.				
Car Insurance	-200						
Fuel	-160						
Electric/Water	-100						
Renter's Ins.	12						
Food / Stuff	-300						
Cable / Internet	-69.95						
GF Car Payment	-400						
Total:	-1697.95						
Net Total:	805.13						
		After 12 month lease:					
		9661.56					
Savings John 1st	Joint after 1yr						
9042.48	9661.56						
Total Savings:							
18704.04							

John is 20 now, has a girlfriend and plans on getting married and the two has a good savings going. How is a budget a headache, or a restriction on a persons finances here.

Gross	1355.2		
Net Household	2503.08	Single	1251.54
Bills:			
Rent	-400		
Phone	-80		
Car Insurance	-200		
Fuel	-160		
Electric/Water	-100		
Renter's Ins	12		
Food / Stuff	-300		
Cable / Internet	-69.95		
GF Car Payment	-400		
Total:	-1697.95		
Net Total:	805.13		
		After 12 month lease:	
			9661.56
Savings John 1st	Joint after 1yr		
9042.48	9661.56		
Total Savings:			
18704.04			

   I will note that in these examples I am leaving out the full picture because items will be covered in later chapters like health insurance, 401k, HSA, raises at work, etc. As you can see though with the first three years even on minimum wage a nice life can be obtained with the correct frame work and foundation. Also the negative was not used for the renter's insurance so offset that by 24 dollars.

   Most people who hate budgets, dislike them because they don't understand them. I did these budgets in a matter of an hour and that is counting breaks, and walking to the work computer to see if there where any notifications. So it is not all that time consuming or complicated. Everyone can do it, and everyone should.

   I have taught two other people some finance lessons. Teenagers both of them. One is married and has a kid, and the other is moving into an apartment soon with his girlfriend.

   They have money and do not struggle, provided they work, and they budget and watch their money. Budgets are awesome when it comes down to planning. Think about it, if you went to build something like a house you would plan it out. If you go to an interview, you plan out your answers usually ahead of time. If you want something you plan on how to obtain it. So it just makes sense to have a financial plan and that begins right here with a budget.

So I will quickly do a few more for John and his wife now, working same job, same pay and few adjustments in life. John sat with his wife discussing the option of a home, and both decided to wait for that until after her car was paid. So here is the breakdown of what happened in balance sheet view, with the given that she has 4 more years of paying on the car.

		John Married						
Gross	1355.2							
Net Household	2503.08							
		After the 5th year they decide since the Girlfriends car is paid, to buy a house and get setup really well.						
Bills:								
Rent	-400							
Phone	-80							
Car Insurance	-200							
Fuel	-160							
Electric / Water	-100							
Renters Ins	-12							
Food / Stuff	-300							
Cable / Internet	-69.95							
GF Car Payment	-400							
Total:	-1721.95							
Net Total	781.13							
John Start	1st year	2nd	3rd	4th	5th	6th	7th	
9042.48	9637.56	9373.56	9373.56	9373.56	9373.56			
Total Savings:								
56174.28								

So a few adjustments here. They decide a 30 year mortgage and put $40,000 down most of their savings. They decide to do the following home.

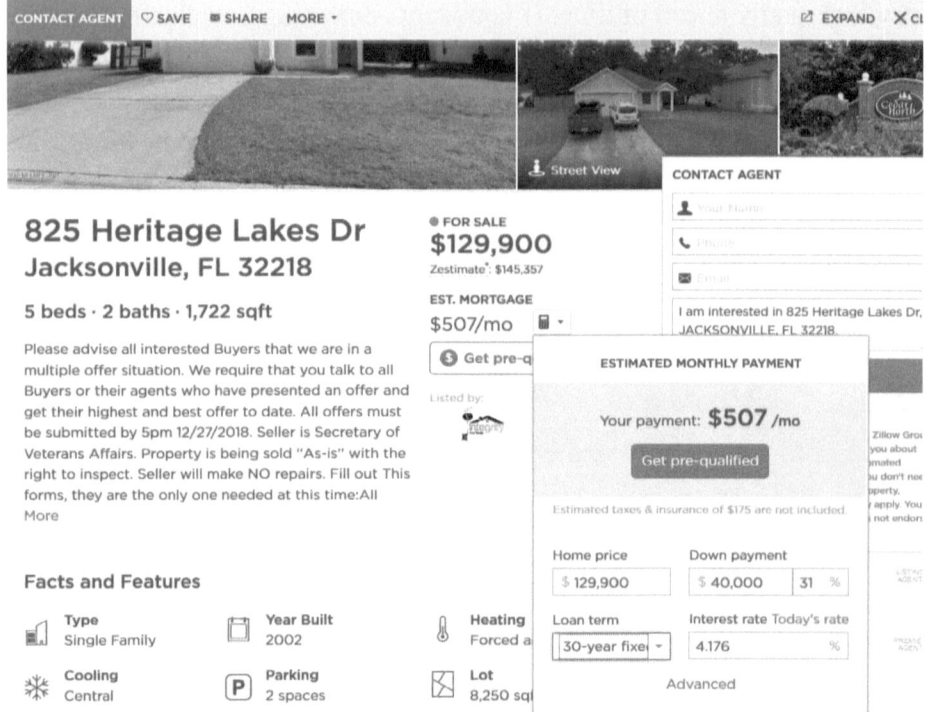

Now let's show the adjustments in budget format. Let's see if they can on minimum wage live comfortable.

John Married

Gross	1355.2									
Net Household	2503.08									
Bills:										
Mortgage	-507									
Phone	-80									
Car Insurance	-200									
Fuel	-200									
Electric / Water	-170									
HOA	-22									
Food / Stuff	-300									
Cable / Internet	-69.95									
Total:	-1548.95									
Net Total	954.13									

John Start	1st year	2nd	3rd	4th	5th	6th	7th	8th	9th	10th
9042.48	9637.56	11449.56	11449.56	11449.56	11449.56	11449.56	11449.56	11449.56	11449.56	11449.56

Total Savings					Total Savings	
56174.28					73422.08	
					Borrowed on House	
					89000	

I would say John is doing well here, mostly because he planned and stuck to the plan. He has a partner that understands the value of a mortgage and he is on minimum wage. He is now 29 Years old. He is in a home, and almost has enough to just pay off the house if he wanted to. Could buy a car if he wanted, or pretty much pay for college classes, or easily raise a kid at this point. Without causing financial disruption. Technically he could do the kid part before, but it will cut into the monthly budget a little and difficult at the start.

Of course he has options too, if he doesn't need bedrooms, he can easily get a house with lower bedrooms and possibly lower cost. I suppose the point I am trying to make is even on minimum wage a person that is financially responsible can have a decent lifestyle. In 30 years of his mortgage if he did nothing else and all things stayed status quo, his savings roughly would be $416,908.88

To end the basics of this chapter I want to say something, that will be explained in later chapters. Sometimes you must extend to contract your costs. This will be fully defined in the chapter about debt and how to crush it.

Just remember you can not live debt free without a budget and a plan.

Chapter 2

Psychology

In the last chapter, I mentioned study everything related to finances, and in this chapter we cover the psychology of money. There is a definite psychological mindset when it comes to money, and if you did not study psychology, then how are you going to reprogram your mind to think about money differently.

Psychology has a very important role to play in your financial world. It shows behavior, choices, and the mental focus on the money. Most adults rank around a B or C at best when it comes to finances, from our scale.

A – Very well versed in financial knowledge

B – Knows more than one strategy when it comes to finances

C – Average. Understands they may have a 401k but does not bother it. Lives from check to check

D – very little financial concepts. Spends all the money on worthless stuff

F – the person that will live off the government and not work.

Most people in life think irrational and only sees a small part that is given instead of being creative or rational, they will jump head first into the fire and suffer the consequences later. Unfortunately finances are less forgiving than most things.

If I present this to you, what would you do? Your dressed up in a suit, and get to a job that has a cafe out by the river. You decide to have a cup of coffee since you have about ten minutes before you actually have to be there for the interview. While sitting down enjoying your coffee a disturbance in the river catches your attention and you see a kid drowning. Would you go save the kid? Needless to say it is the job if you do.

When I ask this of people most answer the same way. You know, my own mother had a bad habit, and I guess at times I do too, in regards to loaning money out. In her circumstance though she really could not afford it, she had nothing built up and was a level C person living from check to check. So did you think of your answer?

Let's say the job was paying about $88,000.00/year. Would you still do it, how about $40,000.00/year still do it? Now what if it was $150,000.00/year. The reason I put money here right now is to make a point. If you decided to save the child, you used irrational behavior and need to readjust your thinking. You took the information I gave and jump into the fire without real thought.

When I ask why would you pass up a job, the general response is you can not put a value on life, or something like that. Some are just the fifteen minutes of fame and hero complex, but most use the ignorant phrase about value of life. Well actually in this case we can. It would be the salary you would have gotten, plus the years you could have put into the job. That is the value you placed on their life.

If you decided to let someone else around save them and go to your job, but it still bothered you, this is what can happen. Instead of saving one life, the incident burned in you, so you take a portion of your pay and setup a foundation to have people patrol the river walk for such things and assist when needed. Now you not only save one child but many. It is more rational to go to the job instead of worrying about one child.

Some of you will be like, but what if that kid died and you could have saved it. Well even more the reason to setup the foundation don't you think. Prevent such things from happening again, better to save more lives vs one life, at least that is what most people say when presented with that scenario.

My point in this questioning is to show how most people will jump head first without a rational thought or a bigger picture of what can be accomplished. It is like going through your financial life without a budget.

You have generational differences as well. The whole aspect of get paid, pay bills, get what is needed, then save if you can is a typical industrial age concept. This is how you can easily fall into the live from check to check. This is looking at money from the aspect of irrational, don't worry most of us were taught that way.

Remember how I keep saying expand to shrink, debt to debt free, sometimes it just takes a simple reverse in thought process to obtain the results wanted. It sounds like a paradox, it sounds irrational, but once you are able to look at a budget and see where these things can occur, it no longer looks like a contradiction but a logical choice.

When I spoke the words to my mother, "Your going to find out you can help no one if you don't take care of yourself first." Those were spoken after she loaned some money out. She found out that this was the case, and one of the reasons she lived from check to check, that and the antiquated style of finances she was doing in the industrial way of thinking.

In order to help other people financially you have to be selfish. It sounds like a contradiction, however I assure you this is the case. The other contradiction is talking to other people about money. This very concept is hard to do as many people that have fallen into a bad path, when talking money and numbers looks at a person as they are taking pride in their finances. Here is the thing though about money everyone needs to understand. Money is only worth the value you put on it, the value the government or world banks put on it. It is essentially worthless if you look at it from it's intrinsic value.

When you realize that, pride disappears, but money does make the world turn as it is said. So an item worthless is so valuable to people. Think of that for a moment, it is a contradiction is it not? Psychologically , though the brain does not like to think in contradictions. The mind when it comes to finances thinks with the emotional brain. It jumps in, it spends on a whim, and it tries to avoid certain things.

Most people want to save, yet they spend the money on things not needed. They spend and spend on a 50" television when a 32" would work just fine. They spend thousands on a state of the art car, when a simple car is fine. The cars both serve the same purpose, to travel back and forth from work or where ever.

Human beings are competitive by nature, jealous by nature, and envious. These are things that need not happen in the financial world. In fact it is best to think of finances with the logic side of the mind, but still keep a little emotion for the creativity aspect.

Think of it in the previous chapter, in the case of John. He could easily go more into debt vs the savings and pay off the girlfriend's car at an accelerated rate. Putting more time for the savings and cutting out more interest that would have been accrued. This would be extending in order to shrink in the amount of bills one has. Before I explained this it sounded illogical, or irrational.

At the real estate association that I went to, a gentlemen stated the following: "It is not about how much money you go in to debt with but how much you can keep". Meaning sometimes debt is a good thing, in order to come out the other side with more money. With John, it would be how much he could keep due to interest being charged on the loan.

Most people do not understand that it is the nickle and dime of interest rates that chew them up and spit them out. Say you had about five major bills, and each bill charged a ten percent annual percent rate. If all the bills were one hundred dollars, you would spend roughly spend four dollars and 16 cents per month or fifty dollars a year on thin air called interest.

The obvious is true as well, if the bill is higher then generally the amount of money wasted on interest rates are generally higher, even if that bill may have a lower interest rate.

Psychologically it is not all that much when a person looks at it, so they pay no mind to it.   They overlook it in the greater scheme of things. They accept interest rates without haggling about them, or without demanding it to be lower if the company wants their business.

Take a car purchase for example, they can easily take your APR and make it lower, but over five to six years you are paying that APR they are making a good profit especially if it is high, and they have hundreds of customers, with car loans. Sounds like highway robbery, but it is on the negotiation during purchase. If you do not like your APR then stop thinking of the finance world as just your luck or there is nothing you can do. Stop looking at the small things as small things, and consider the bigger picture it plays.

With the psychology of finance nothing is ever out of reach with some negotiation, and everything can be negotiated for the best optimal deal. When you quit accepting what is given to you, and realize you have power, you start reprogramming your psyche to become more inline with the financial world. You can even go a step further and say take advantage of the financially weak, and bolster your position in your own finances. However, I would advise against that unless you plan on being a banker, or loan manager or something like that. I am more of a teacher of finance and want to see everyone understand the financial world that is filled with sharks.

I would say that sharks are those out there that have the ability to help a person but chooses to use that ability to take advantage of a person. If you think about it, sometimes a person with money will help invest into a company or loan money and then they take more than what they should. These are sharks. A person should get something out of it, but there is a limitation as to acceptable and advantage.

Generally the natural psychology of a human is to initially trust someone at face value, however in the financial world it is better to question everyone and look at the data. It is also natural to try to gain as much out of a situation as possible. Psychologically this is fine to a point, you should gain in things, but just remember there is such a thing as too much and greed.

You should base all things off data mostly and creativity. Emotions really should not play a part in your finances. Emotions create the giving away of money to those that will not pay it back, or buying something for someone that is not willing to learn how to handle their money. The list goes on, but those are emotions that cause that, and some people are really good at pulling on the heart strings.

If you don't have several thousand's of dollars in savings, then by data you should not loan money. You have to look at it this way, if you have money in the bank but the bills have not cleared and you would not have enough to cover the loan, you end up short on cash. However, if you have money for the bills that have not cleared and a thousand dollars in the bank, you could cover ten or twenty dollars in a loan.

If a person comes and gives you the following sob story, you have to give them credit for their ability to manipulate the human altruism. "My son's birthday is today, and I am freaking out because I can not afford to get him a cake. I am stressed out and have no hope of salvaging the 8 year old's birthday. If only someone could help me out."

Here is the thing, even if the person is a friend, no should be your answer, break out of the altruistic nature that is programmed into you. First and foremost you must take care of self. Tell the person to ask their parents from both sides for cash. Ask them to look at their bank account and wallet as proof of lack of funds. If they are truly hard up, they should have no issues showing you this. Tell the person to ask the other parent for help. With every question and pointing out the issue here, you find they go away pretty quick. Especially when you ask about looking into their accounts, and seeing their budgets.

Personally, I do not see how a person can live like that, never having money and leeching off friends. My suggestion is if you have a friend like that, either learn to say no always, or get rid of them before they pull you into the bankrupt house.

Personally, I have a rule to handle my altruism. I will loan money to a person once, and will not do it again, unless the loan is repaid in full. If it isn't I will never loan again to that person. The only reason I can do this is because I have capital setup for such things. I don't charge interest to the friends.

Another tactic to overcome is the tactic of reciprocity. Which means the person gets you something, and you feel the need to reciprocate and get them something or owe them something. This is non-existing in the financial world.

If you think about it in game theory, which is actually more intense subject field than people realize, reciprocity is on the level of zero-sum game. It gives and takes, and tries to equal zero which will not happen when the reset happens one will always give and another always take, there is not equality in this exchange. It is not a very beneficial aspect when it comes down to it, but it is human nature.

I will say this though, if you are truly interested in finances, it would be beneficial to learn some game theory even if it is generalized knowledge. Game theory can help in forming strategies, and determine what needs to happen depending on the game being played. Which I will say is more psychological than anything else.

Chapter 3

Self Investment

The first investment a person will every make is the investment into themselves. This investment could very well be the most rewarding investment that keeps paying over time. Congratulations, just reading this book is part of learning and investing into something that will be there long after all the other investments and something you will continually use, which is knowledge.

Most young people today do not even realize that their general schooling is a step into self investing. Going to college or learning a skill after that is another step to the self investment portfolio.

Knowledge is pretty much like a portfolio, if you invest only in one area, you can end up hurting yourself, but if you diversify the portfolio it allows more growth and options later on.

Let's take a something that seems very non-important like taking a cooking class. Seems like nothing to do with your corporate job, however later on, you loose that corporate job and decide you like cooking, so you have some skills to obtain that beginning chef or cook job that you saw. Now you are making money again, but under a whole different portfolio skill.

Things that seem unimportant really can come back full circle, plus just having the knowledge in areas that seem non-important at the time, is just adding to your portfolio of self investments.

Here is a free way to expand your portfolio, especially if you ever plan on buying a home. If your a male or female it is still a good idea to expand knowledge. Home Depot offers free DIY classes on Saturday that you can take and learn skills to help you with your home when you get one, or if you already have one. It provides a free portfolio item into your self investment, well kind of free, it is only paid with time.

You can find many classes around your own town for free or for small fees. All you have to do is search in a search engine. Of course any knowledge you obtain is just more you can place in your own self investment portfolio.

Planning on buying a house, well before you do join the local Real Estate Investment Association or REIA. Typically these will have classes in order to show you what to look for, what to expect, how to look for issues, and what you can expect from a investor aspect, which when you buy your home, it truly is an investment. Something like this also can help if you ever wanted to make money through real estate either flipping or renting out the home.

One thing I will have to say though, is don't believe everything you see on television like the flip this house, or any of that. They usually do not show the whole story, and some REIA tries to sell systems, don't fall for those as well. Usually, unless your serious it is a waste of money, and if you are serious you will form your own system, not use a system someone else created.

Learning about money and financial strategies may not sound like all that much of an investment, but in the long run, when you decide to learn and test things out, and adjust things when needed, you will find that knowledge is the true essence of power and the true essence of success.

As like in the last chapter about psychology, it is beneficial to take some classes or read a little upon psychology, so one can see how to change a thought process or what to look for when dealing with others. Along with psychology, that is a subset of the art is learning how to read people and micro-expressions. I would advise anyone wanting to deal with others in a financial aspect to pick up as many books from Paul Ekman. Another skill that will help along the way.

Learning game theory for example will help assess how to price things, what will happen in certain circumstances, and what the outcome probability will be if certain things or strategies are done. It really is a complex system, with some interesting concepts.

Finance world is a giant world, with many concepts and ideas behind it. You have two sides of the world, personal finance and business finance. Each have sub sections under them like book-keeping, both have it but they are done so much differently on a basic scale.

So learning both sides just increases the portfolio, and even though done differently it does not mean the way business does things could not be used on personal side, it can. I mention this because if your going to invest in yourself, you need to understand that no matter what one can not 100% know or retain everything about every topic, but you can become very proficient without 100% of the topic.

Everyone regardless of life, environment, or choices, starts out with the choice of self investment. Starting at school, from there they have a choice on what to start putting into their own self portfolio. Some decide to build it with great diversity, and others choose to ignore it. Some choose to specialize, and others decide to generalize. You only get out of self investing as much as you put into it.

Understanding that as you go through your life, you will have wins and losses, but the real goal is to take part in the self investment of knowledge so when losses occur, you loose as little as possible. To understand an investments actual worth, the very first investment one should choose is the most priceless.

The housing market is a great example of this, sellers sell high, buyers buy low, and it all comes down to understanding the house your buying. Without previous knowledge you could be overpaying for the investment. Things that could be fixed before purchase are now your responsibility due to the lack of knowledge of what to look for.

The very first investment, being your knowledge take time, but more than that it takes courage and dedication. Courage to obtain the knowledge and dedication with always learning more. This very nature is the one that sticks with you through all other investments. Courage to face the fear, courage to loose money, or make money, courage to try. The dedication comes in on sticking with the decisions and seeing them through or pulling out when the line is crossed. Dedicating yourself to continually to watch the investments.

If you must have fear when it comes to investments, be afraid of being stagnant or non-moving. If the move is to store up a bundle and waiting for a good opportunity, your still moving stuff around, and it is not being stagnant, it has a purpose, just not ready to be used yet.

Fear treading water and barely keeping your head above the water. This life style is much more difficult and easy to sink into, especially if that is how you were taught.

There really is not much more I can say about self investing. You invest in yourself and you get the rewards, it really is simple. Many people fear that part. You do not have to go to college or anything like that unless you wanted to, however there are always ways to learn and invest in yourself. Just remember to never get discouraged and keep trying.

Chapter 4

Debt

The old adage goes, "It takes money to make money." Usually this comes in the form of debt. Debt is a bad thing right? Is it? Could you think of times Debt is a good thing, or can help vs hurt?

Most people knows debt very well, in fact many are being eaten up by debt, or very close to it. Debt is what you make it though, and it is as bad or as good as one wishes it to be. Later on, strategies will be shown that can change your idea about debt, but until then, let's see what we can do in order to change your aspect on debt.

Think about how most people handle bills, how even you may be handling bills. Take a paycheck, pay what is needed at the beginning of the month, try to save, and pretty much have very little left to put into savings. Then spend the rest, ending up broke by the next paycheck. This is the industrial age of financing. Then the second check you repeat the process.

It is an old outdated way of looking at finances depending what a person has built so far. However, since this is what is normal, we will have to get a loan for a car, home, etc. There are many reasons for debt, and usually many people have the common debts.

We hate the bill, but without that bank or angel investing in you, then those items you would not have. We love having a car, just not the bill of the loan. We love having a home, but not the bill. We end up living from check to check and so we hate the bills, the debt.

What if we look at it from this aspect. Does anyone right now have about 20,000 – 30,000 expendable income to just buy a car outright? Most people do not, if you do, then why are you reading this book? The reading this book was a joke, please continue reading. I would enjoy your company as I go through this experience.

So here is a question, would you like debt if you were the one loaning the money? Would you like interest rates if you were the one helping someone out and getting some money for loaning your money to them?

This goes back to the psychology of money, you loan friends money all the time, and they pay you back, but did your money really do anything for you? Did you gain anything in the exchange, except the temporary loss of your money?

However, if you loan your friend money and tell them, if you loan them $100.00 then you want a 5% interest rate as well. Then they pay you back $105.00, did your money do something different? Would you be happier making the $5.00 and helping a friend? Would it be more fair exchange on that level?

Utility comes into play when you deal with finances and psychology. You utility should not cost you, but help you.

Utility – Noun - With regard to making decisions and economic theory, the subjective worth of some result to a person in industrial and establishment psychology

In general, most people when it comes to decisions and money the thought of utility is lacking. The worth is subjugated to the emotion not to the practical. In essence you hate debt because of practicality, you focus on emotion. Debt is no saint, but it is no demon either. It is what you make it.

Debt can spiral out of control if you do not return to the basics, and save for a rainy day. If the basics is not followed then it is easy to do one loan after another and end up owing more than you make. If this happens you end up sinking the boat. Which means probably a bankruptcy on the books, which is no fun climbing back from that.

Debt though is needed to build FICO, a scoring system for credit and loans. It is a number used to give rates to those borrowing money. Sometimes, though like in the case of Rainsoft or should I say Aqua Financing, they care less about FICO and give the highest rate they can without going to the usury laws.

Usury laws exist but many people do not even know what they are, and it is different per state. So in the case of John in chapter 1, he lives in Florida. The law in Florida states the following:

All contracts for the payment of interest upon any loan, advance of money, line of credit, or forbearance to enforce the collection of any debt, or upon any obligation whatever, at a higher rate of interest than the equivalent of 18 percent per annum simple interest are hereby declared usurious. However, if such loan, advance of money, line of credit, forbearance to enforce the collection of a debt, or obligation exceeds $500,000 in amount or value, then no contract to pay interest thereon is usurious unless the rate of interest exceeds the rate prescribed in s. 687.071

So what do we now know about debt and FICO. Well if you have a good credit score and the highest percentage a person can charge in Florida is 18% for anything up to $500,000.00 and a place is trying to sell you something for 17.99%, you should walk away from this offer. In fact unless you have horrible credit or not credit you should walk away and go to your bank instead.

Never look at debt as you have no choice, you always have a choice and you should always take the negotiating initiative. Never feel like you can not negotiate terms, this is how people really take advantage of you. You can always negotiate or walk away and try a different avenue. If you really want help but everyone turns you away or tries to overcharge you, then try something like lending club, where personal lenders help fund a loan, that you pay back.

Most people get messed up by loans, because they do not know the laws for one, and forget the negotiating initiative. Most people loose in Credit score as well due to the lack of knowledge between what is called a hard pull, and a soft pull.

A **hard credit pull** or **hard credit** inquiry is when a bank or lender **pulls** your **credit** report and **credit** score to determine whether or not you meet the requirements for them to lend you money. A **hard credit pull** will reduce your **credit** score slightly.

A **soft** inquiry, sometimes referred to as a **soft pull**, is made on your **credit** report whenever you check your **credit** report, a business checks your **credit** report for promotional purposes, or a business you already have an account with checks your **credit** report.

So if your buying a car for example and your shopping around, tell them to only pull a soft report instead of a hard pull. Do this until you have a working deal, and start the negotiation early on. Tell them that they can pull a soft report and that you want the best possible options, especially if you have great credit. Pretty much the initiative is really on your side when you have a great score.

Never accept the first offer, never ever do this. Make them bite into their profits a little, why should you have no choice in how much profit they make from you? Think of it this way, and remember you may have to walk a couple of times, but patience and determination will get your the best possible deals.

Most people hate debt, because they feel like they were bent over a barrel, and had no choice. They did not take the negotiation initiative, did not state to only soft pull until a preliminary deal was made, and they forgot their laws and where in the law their score would fit. This is typical because no one really teaches this, and no one really mentions it.

Let's talk about FICO and why it is important and how it is calculated a little. FICO although not a great way to determine the risk of loan to person it is the best we have right now, until "True Score" or whatever they are going to call it comes out fully. FICO is calculated with the following weights generally, but no one really knows if they follow this strictly.

• Payment History	35.00%
• Amount of debt	30.00%
• Length of credit history	15.00%
• Amount of new credit	10.00%
• Credit mix	10.00%

Exceptional	800-850
Very Good	740-799
Good	670-739
Fair	580-669
Poor	300-579

Part of good debt control is understanding your FICO, and

understanding your credit scores, debt to income ratios, and payment being late or on time. All these play in part to handle the best outcome for debt.

The other part that matters is what type of loan is it that you are going for? Some fields are generalized, while others can be fully negotiated. Think of a house, the rates are impacted by FICO, but also by market, same with car. However, a loan for kitchen remodel can and should be negotiated, and if they do not want to negotiate walk and go with another person that is willing to work with you. You will find that as soon as you start to walk most of them will offer x offer just for you, or ask you to let them talk to the finance depart real quick.

The same practice though can be used for the car loans as well. You would be amused at the eagerness of a car salesman to get rid of a car. If you think about it financially, they have to pay on a car until it sells, so they truly want to get rid of it, even if it means making a small profit, however most people do not want to negotiate and use the walk away ability to force negotiation.

So what reasons do you want to pay bills on time for? In the United States many people either has a bad payment, or defaulted medical bill. The number is staggering. It hurts credit, and hurts the chances of a lender allowing you to borrow their money. It drops your score, and it is a pain to recover from. As they say, one bad thing is harder to recover from than a thousand good things. In the credit world this is even more so.

What to do if something is gone to collections? The first thing is to negotiate a payoff price, offer 25% of the bill in writing and then work your way up to 50% but nothing more. When doing this all in writing make sure you also mention that the pay off also requires removal from credit reporting of all three major score holders. The three major Credit companies are Trans Union, Equifax, and Experian here in the United

States. If you are in a different country, you should know who your reporters are for credit.

If you look at debt as a a bad thing, or as a thing that can totally destroy your finances, you will go forward very slowly, however if you educate yourself about debt and how to manage it, then it can increase your potential and speed of getting to a point in your financial life that you can pretty much laugh when a person says it depends on your credit report.

Just remember debt is not a competition, you should never live beyond your means, your budget and your income. If you constantly see a friend get something new or flashy, it does not mean that you should as well. In fact, the first question in your own mind is how did they afford it, what does the finances look like for them to afford such a gadget, and how much debt did they incur getting it. Remember, nothing is free and money going out, takes away from money you keep. It also provides less for the overall financial freedom you are shooting for.

Finances remind me about the old fable about the grasshopper and squirrel. Sacrifice now for enjoyment later, or sacrifice now and hurt later. If you want to compete with the friends, neighbors, or strangers, well nothing will be able to assist in getting the finances on the write path, just remember it is your debt, your credit and no one else is responsible for it.

Chapter 5

Planning and Essentials

So what is meant by planning? What are essentials? Planning involves a different spin on budgets, and essentials really means knowledge. The essential knowledge before starting an endeavor, never jump into something you do not fully know something about, or understand the majority of the situation.

So let's start with planning, some people call them financial calendars, or a road map for future money. It contains some what a minimum budget details, and then a calendar based of month, then what the plans are for the future money. This tool is to stick to a plan, a plan that is viewed each month at the very least, or more if you enjoy looking at what the future money will be doing.

In the example we are about to show, is real life data, a scenario I did as a test, or a case study in the financial studies based off my income and bills.

	A	B	C	D	E	F
1	Paycheck	2000	Monthly	4000	Heloc Start	2699.59
2			Actual	2900		
3						
4						
5						
6	Month	HELOC Tracking			House Principal Tracking	
7	Dec 2018	599.59			63936.72	
8	Jan 2019	0			63580.1	
9	Feb 2019	2800			61223.48	
10	Mar 2019	700			60866.86	
11	Apr 2019	0			60510.24	
12	May 2019	2800			58153.62	
13	Jun 2019	700			57797	
14	Jul 2019	0			57440.38	
15	Aug 2019	2800			55083.76	
16	Sep 2019	700			54727.14	
17	Oct 2019	0			54370.52	
18	Nov 2019	2800			52013.9	
19	Dec 2019	700			51657.28	
20	Jan 2020	0			51300.66	
21	Feb 2020	2800			48944.04	
22	Mar 2020	700			48587.42	
23	Apr 2020	0			48230.8	
24	May 2020	2800			45874.18	
25	Jun 2020	700			45517.56	
26	Jul 2020	0			45160.94	
27	Aug 2020	2800			42804.32	
28	Sep 2020	700			42447.7	
29	Oct 2020	0			42091.08	
30	Nov 2020	2800			39734.46	
31	Dec 2020	700			39377.84	

G	H	I	J	K
	CC	211.75		Car
	Average / Month	800		Principal
		Car Principal		
		30647.21		
		30278.94		
		29910.67		
		29542.4		
		29174.13		
		28805.86		
		28437.59		
		28069.32		
		27701.05		
		27332.78		
		26964.51		
		26596.24		
		26227.97		
		25859.7		
		25491.43		
		25123.16		
		24754.89		
		24386.62		
		24018.35		
		23650.08		
		23281.81		
		22913.54		
		22545.27		
		22177		
		21808.73		

L	M	N	O
31015.48		House	64293.34
368.27		Normal Pay Princ	356.62
Savings			
3500	x		
4040	x		
4540			
5040			
5540			
6040			
6540			
7040			
7540			
8040			
8540			
9040			
9540			
10040			
10540			
11040			
11540			
12040			
12540			
13040			
13540			
14040			
14540			
15040			
15540			

So what is this. I put in the essential details of the income, the liabilities, the payment structures (interest, principal, etc) at the top of the spreadsheet. Then you can calculate what happens if you have extra money and put toward a principal, and how long it would take to pay off a debt.

This example uses a strategy that I will be going over in future chapters. For lack of a better name, I refer to it as leveraging, but that will occur in another chapter. The result of this practice is now you have a budget and a road map of what your money can do in future months.

It allows one to determine what the money can actually accomplish when set up against a debt, and allows you to mostly stick with the plan. There are some things that will adjust it slightly, but it is not a plan written completely in stone, but more of a guide. If you have to take a detour, simply adjust it and then try to follow it. The calendar or road map can be a little flexible if you have no choice but to alter it. The trick though is to try not to alter the plan by too much or too often.

In the example above, the plan is to pay $2000.00 down on the principal every quarter on the mortgage principal only. Still paying the regular bill when it comes in. Shifting the debt to the HELOC, which can then be paid off in 2 months at a 4% interest rate. Why do this? It cuts the overall interest rate from the house which has more time to collect.

Remaining Loan Balance	Current Term / Rate
$61,567.45	**15 years / 2.99%**

Extra Payment Savings

Extra Principal Paid:	**$4,462.00**
Interest Saved:	**$2,015.44**
Payments Saved:	**12**
Current Loan Maturity:	**9/1/2030**

If you see it, paying on the principal in this manner has essentially save a years worth of payment. You can also see that I only recently started on their house in this manner.

This is one application that can be done with calendars, this was tested previously on other debts to clear them out. Essentially though a calendar is a great tool to use to manage the money of the future and determine the route your are on. Then compare it to budgets and see how well your are sticking to the calendar. A checks and balances system for the financial world, well one of them.

Having the essential knowledge on how to do something, and what happens will help a person make a significant educated decision based off data, instead of emotion, or a whim. It is the core of good finances, instead of following a get rich quick scheme and possibly loosing money on a non-knowledgeable field.

It would be essentially a bad move for me to just jump into bonds at the moment because I do not have enough knowledge in them. Same thing is true into the Real Estate Flipping market. If you do not feel you have enough knowledge in a field, then do not jump into it. Test the waters by gaining the knowledge. Though I may have some knowledge in the Real Estate Investing, I am still not comfortable with it, so I avoid it. Money not spent is money not lost.

Before you read a book about investing in housing, or in the stock market, it is best to make sure you fully understand the systems in place, and then question it. Some people write books on how to do things, and then it fails. The leveraged system I spent years questioning before I put it into practice, I questioned it, went through different scenarios, then attempted it as a case study. The leveraged system is not for everyone, and only for the financially disciplined. The rewards though are great.

Please understand there are books out there that have great information but none of them are a get rich quick solution, and some of the data has a serious risk value to them, and a serious fault in not telling you that. This book, when we get to the strategies will have a set risk value to it as well, however it is nominal, and I will explain when a risk is involved and how it is neutralized as much as possible. However, many authors do not do this sufficiently.

You also want to avoid all the make money with no work schemes, or the work from home with this system. Here is what I came to the conclusion of when I investigated these, which I wish I hadn't. They end up selling you on a pyramid scheme, or a system they have to help them get money, you essentially become a sales person, and then they sell your information in a list to other people that do the same thing. They essentially make money off your information. Then you get endless spam calls. I have started selling religion to the spam callers, it is funny when they hang up. I sell them Taoism, Christianity, Islam, pretty much any religion I am feeling like talking about that day. I don't even let them get to their pitch.

If you see a website, or hear of a speaker offering you a system to make money, avoid it, it is only a way for them to make money, while you may make some on their system, there is a reason they are offering their systems, it is loosing steam and needs people to give it fuel.

Take the flipping of houses for example, they teach you a system, but they offer to loan you money in order to do it, then collect an interest rate, and then the fee for the information up front. It really is a rip off, because you can really come up with all this information by joining a local REIA and going to free classes, then there is a luck value in it, or a time value. It is a lot more work than people realize, and if you divide that time, with the payout, most times it is not worth it. Some people can make it worth it, but not everyone.

What does this have to do with the essentials, well I am pretty much saying don't be a sucker, and also understand your limitations. Gain knowledge and factor in the data and limitations before you decide to do something.

In financial world the best way to something is usually by data, and doing the basics, then expanding the basics and knowledge. A primary example of this is making a budget, knowing the terms, understanding the mathematical formulas which are not that difficult. Calendars, and tracking, and understanding data is important, not emotional aspects. Planning your money is the most important aspect of it all, watching, calculating, and having a plan for it, allows one to control how much of that money is allowed to trickle away.

So what is considered essential and planning, budgets, excel or spreadsheet knowledge, reconciling accounts, calendars, and just basic math (although a calculator helps in the math area). Any financial person that you run across that does not have at the very least a basic calculator, run, and I am not talking about the computer calculator, an old school regular calculator. This shows you that they relay on various methods to get to a result not just a computerized aspect.

The very concept of having your money make you money is part of the financially planning aspect, 401k, lending, bonds, stock, renting, land lording, etc. You do not need to understand the full concept of such things at the beginning, or even as you go along life, but understand they term, general idea of what they are and that at some point that one will need to have more than one basket if retirement and financial freedom is every going to be accomplished.

Personal finance can be planned but it is also fluid, you can be a month behind your plan or even end up ahead of your plan, either way it should not derail your plans. Just know that things come up, and it is the very reason we plan on having that rainy day fund, but it also means that we have to adjust and change things a little in order to validate the change and schedules.

Chapter 6

The Ability to Walk Away

So before we go much father into different concepts of money, I must stress the ability to walk away from things in the financial aspect. There will be times in life where you may have to simply cut your loss and move to a different venture, or put the money toward something else.

The first thing I would like to point out in this chapter is when you deal with financial information or financial deals, I have a golden rule for everyone to learn.

Do Not Enter into a financial agreement with a family member for any reason. If you do then realize that there will be times when you have to walk away before the agreement puts you into a jeopardized situation.

It doesn't just happen with family, in certain circumstances you will have the ability to walk away. For example vehicles that end up as lemons, or a program you joined that is not providing you with what you expected. These are just a few things that can lead a person to just walk away.

Always walk away from the idea of failing, failure only happens when you quit trying, or quit asking how to do something better, failure does not happen when you stumble, or when something goes wrong. Things that set you back or make you stumble are going to happen, but walk away from quitting and from failing.

Walking away does not mean quit, it means to walk away from a bad situation in order to turn it to a better one. Walking away from a stock or a mutual fund for a better option. Walking away from a bad deal in order to mitigate the negative financial impact it has. Essentially, you are correcting a drain, or an issue, and walking away from that issue, even though the possibility of loss of money occurred, it is still about how much you keep, and if something continues to drain finances then you must decide your risk appetite and walk away when it is hit.

In personal finance there are always times you get off track, always something that may happen to derail the plan. However; it is the disciplined and the ones hungry that will not let it stop them from getting back on track. It is the ability to walk away from that feeling of hopelessness or despair and turn it into something more productive.

There was this student that came to learn about credit and what could be done. The situation is like this, he moved north from Florida for a job, that had the potential to eventually pay more. Before the move, the bills were taken care of and did not have to worry about money. He moved up north for a little less money, but with potential to make more, unfortunately he had to pay for his own move.

Unfortunately the potential never came through, and a move back was performed, and it took more money to move back. I am sure you can see how this stress on the finances of the man goes, it puts a strain on the finances that can almost break a person.

For three years roughly the man has struggled, his credit was being messed up, and he was for lack of better reference drowning. The one thing this man had that many do not have is the craving and determination to do better, to overcome the situation, however little things were missing, knowledge, and he was slowly gaining that by reading and gaining information from people.

When we started talking about finance and credit and what could be done, the man become very motivated to try some things we talked about, and was very quick to move on certain aspects for the financial world. One of the most driven people that I have met, after talking with them about the world of money, and what could be accomplished. He quickly fixed multiple issues with the credit report, reduced certain payments, removed others, and increased his score almost immediately.

This is a prime example of a driven person that never gave up, he walked away from the feeling of despair and walked away from the idea of being beaten down by our society standards.

Motivation and mindset is a key to the financial world, if you ever played a game you realize you always want a higher score. My students, and myself usually treat our net worth along the same lines, as a games high score. The players in this game, only yourself. You try to beat yourself, not anyone else.

My students and I always talk about money, and we are not afraid to share what we have in the terms of high score with each other. We can do this because we are not in competition with each other but because we want to get input on how we can do something better, or if there is a venture that worked for someone else that we could get in on. At no point do we ever feel like it is a competition. Why would we the high score is just a game to us.

The concept of keeping finances a secret is good, however, if you trust someone or belong to a group of people that strive to push each other into a better direction, then keeping money secret is more detrimental than beneficial. If you hide what you have, how is someone going to give you advice on what can be accomplished with what you have, or how to build even more than what you have.

I have walked away from competing with others, and when I show people my finances and where they are, it is in a humble way, and with the concept that they can accomplish what I have and more. It is to show that even though I am doing well, it is not impossible for anyone to do.

Walking away from competition with others and toward competition with yourself, works for the students and for myself. However, I am not saying to just go out and sharing your financial data with just anyone, in fact for the most part it should be kept secret, but if your building an investment group, or building a group of people that love money, then you can get more by sharing amounts than by hiding it.

This chapter may have been one of the shorter chapters in this book, but please understand it is one of the most important, and one with the most power message. Never give up, and never be afraid to walk away from something.

Chapter 7

The Multi-Disciplines of Finance

In this chapter we will go over an overview of the multiple disciplines of the financial world. We will cover each one briefly as a definition aspect or function aspect of the financial world. Take for a moment and think about financial world as just the concept of reality, and the disciplines the multiple worlds of that reality. Each one is in itself, a world all to it's own. Things can become very complicated depending on what world you are jumping to. Savings for example is going to function much different than lending or stock market plays.

In each of these disciplines some things need to be taken into some consideration. Security being one of the most vital, risk appetite, risk assessment, and potential. These are a few but not all the items to take into consideration with each discipline.

So the disciplines are as follows:

1. **Savings** – Pretty much a rainy day fund, and if you do well with it it can also help in retirement. It is pretty much your bank account. The opposite of this is spending.

2. **Stocks** – This is where you buy and sell company portions in order to create capital.

3. **IRA's** – This is commonly known as retirement or 401k, if your in the government it is a 457. There are many flavors of these but most of them work along the same way. Pensions as well but they are very different but they fit in

the same discipline.

4. **Loans** – This area has two different functions, think of it as Client and Provider, and you can exist on either side or both at the same time.

5. **Credit** – This is a scoring system, and treated differently than loans, because even though those loans may impact the scoring, it is in itself a world all to it's own.

6. **Real Estate** – Investing into real estate as a person that fixes and flips or as a land lord. Both have advantages and disadvantages.

7. **Bonds** – These are notes/contracts of indebtedness to you as the lender.

8. **CD** – Certificate of Deposits. There are several strategies surrounding this, but essentially it is a saving you don't plan on touching for an increase in interest earned or dividend if you with to use that term.

9. **Taxes** – A world all to it's own. The most despised aspect of finance there is.

10. **HSA type accounts** – Tax differed medical accounts.

These are the most common disciplines. There may be some more or some sub-disciplines that fit along these one but this should cover the general aspect of financial world.

The trick here is to realize that not one alone can help you build a financial independence. Let us go into what it means for financial independence or FI. FI is calculated by doing the following:

FI# = Yearly spending / SWR (do 4%)

Then you take the FI# and subtract what you already have saved, divided by the amount you save in a year.

Years to FI = FI#-Saved / Amount saved in a year

This is where your budget skills can really come into play and help you get FI quickly or at the very least determine the calculation on how long before FI. Calculating my FI I see 9 years before I can hit FI. Now this number can fluctuate due to expenses and due to current plans. For example the finances in 4 years will take a shift from the expenditures by $1000.00 a month or $12,000.00 a year due to the mortgage and truck payment being completed. Which at time the spending a year would shrink from $21,441.60 to a measly $4,599.36 without calculating taxes on the house or the home owners insurance.

Take out the debt shrinks your time to get to FI drastically. Once finished with the debt, try not to get back into the debt if at all possible. Plus it is always best to have more money than your FI number, just for special occasions, or for spare spending. Once your FI it does not mean your free to go on a spending spree, it means that if you focused on bills then you would be good, however the more you spend the more you will need.

So that is FI, and that should be the goal of every person, how to become fundamentally free from financial burdens. This is where some of the basics like budgeting and the multi-disciplines of finances come into play.

Savings

So let's start with the aspect of savings shall we and we will go through all the disciplines that are listed. A savings account is actually needed however if you ever plan on retirement it is not the best option.

The reason for savings is for those unexpected expenditures, the rainy day funding. Life has many rainy days it seems, however, the financial minded will plan for these and will not suffer too much when they occur.

The issue with a savings account is the low interest you earn on it. It is pathetic at the interest rate you get for the banks to hold and use your money. It is not a very financial benefit for an investor or for a financially minded person. Some of the highest yielding savings accounts are 2.30% or 2.50%. You should however read the fine print, usually these percentages are on a high dollar amount. Typically banks will do something like 0.08% and below, which you can see how pathetic this is.

Especially when they take the money you have them hold, invest it, then turn it around for billions of dollars of profit, but then only give you a chump change amount for using it for such actions. This is how banks and insurance companies work to make a profit.

The easy solution, put the majority of money elsewhere, keep just a small rainy day fund available. Don't let the banks keep making money off you and not paying you enough to hold your money. Just keep enough in there to handle so much time unemployed, the common amount is 6 months, however I would suggest a year or build to it before cutting the account off and putting it elsewhere. For $20,000 at a 0.03% you would make $6.00 a month. Does that sound like it is a good investment to you? It sure doesn't to me.

Stocks

Stocks are very volatile, they go up and down drastically. You generally would fall into 2 types of traders. The type that goes for the long term investments, ones that believe in a company and collects dividends from those bets. Then there is the type that go with trends and day trade, attempting to make profits off sales and buys. Myself since I do not have the time, I became the prior type. Stocks are fun though as you actually own a fraction all though be it fundamentally low percentage of the company.

I am not here to teach stocks because they are very volatile and I am not going to be held responsible for anyone getting into something with out research, however I am very satisfied with the stocks I own. I have $950.00 in the market at this time, and I get roughly $30.00 in dividends a year. That is almost ten times the amount a bank would give me.

Some things you will need to understand about stocks though is that it can sway depending on what our government does, the elite tend to sway the market when say the President puts a tariff or threatens a tariff on a country, the sad thing is that these people are just throwing a temper tantrum, so before you pull out of an option or buy more understand why the market is shifting, chances are it will come right back.

The same is true like in 2008 when companies went out of business, due to the banking fiasco that the government allowed to happen. I knew a person that would not listen to many people and the 401k was in Lehman Brothers. Once it went down so far he still didn't want to listen and put his 401k into safe position, in which case he lost everything. Sometimes you must take a loss in order to keep the main amount. When playing the stock market don't get too greedy but don't be too proud to pull the plug on an option that is loosing money.

IRA's

This is where the majority of American's hold their retirement. This also plays on the stock market however each fund is a mix of many companies on the market, and is managed by a fund manager, in most 401k type IRA. The great thing about these are the company you work for will match and it is pre-tax money. Pre-tax means that taxes are not hitting that money until retirement. There are tricks here to help, because who knows what the taxes will be like in the future. Especially with the way our government and the Democrats want free things for all people, which means more taxation and that would hurt retirement plans in the future.

You also have something called a Roth IRA which is post tax, meaning the government can not tax it in the future because they already did. This is where the trick comes to play, about 5 years before retirement move the money into Roth IRA that way you have been taxed once. What this does is pay out all the taxes at once instead of per distribution through retirement. In other words pay the government once for all the tax avoidance you acquired through the years under 401k.

Then there is something called a self directed IRA with is pretax as well, however this type of IRA will allow a wider range of investments including real estate, however accessing the money and rules around it is a little more strict, you can essentially use these types for real estate flipping for example.

Loans

Everyone in the world understands the term loans and how they can cost money. However, not many people understand loans well enough to know you can make money from loans by becoming the loaner instead of the receiver of the loan. It is not all that difficult to perform now either. Loan money even to a friend, write up a simple contract that calculates the interest rate and then have them sign the contract and have it notarized. That is one way, however a more efficient way is to visit a place called lending club.

The only thing I can say negative about this is, if your not careful you can have people that pay late. The great benefit is that with the smallest amount being $25.00 per loan bid, even if they do not pay your not out much, however you don't claim much either if your not betting some on them paying.

The seed amount was $1100.00 which got about 10 notes at various amounts. The portfolio states I get roughly around $39.13 a month of principle and interest. I take the money I get in principle and interest and reinvest into a new note. Generally these loans are for 3 years and every month I can purchase a new note at $25.00. Now this does not sound like a lot, however when the account feeds itself enough the default amount will raise to $50.00 then more.

You can see how this can grow, I should hope. The great thing is, if you toy with programming languages and API, the site has an API. You could essentially plug into it and form a program that will do all the checks and trades for you. Leaving it as a hands off system for investing.

Some things to understand about this type of investing would be calculating percentages, FICO, Credit, and the term delinquent. Avoid delinquent people if at all possible. They may give you a better percentage of interest, however they also are more apt to miss a payment or be late.

Currently with 18 notes total I get roughly a 9% growth on the money, this is actually way better than the bank. Although the account has 1 person that is constantly late, it is not bad at all. The program that was built will do a formula and take into consideration a blacklist of people not to loan to again. So you can see how versatile this system can be. Plus it is another stream of income, having money make money with little to no intervention from my part.

Credit

This was touched up on in a previous chapter, but remember to pay attention to your Credit Score and record, it becomes vital if money is ever to be loaned to you, also it becomes vital to understand it if you are going to loan anyone money as well. The American Society revolves on Credit, we just can't help it, we need money and we never have enough, especially starting out.

Just remember nothing over 30% of loan amount to be used, and that credit can be detrimental if not handled correctly, but if handled right it could be just as pleasurable, eventually the goal would be to transition from a person that uses credit for help to a person that uses credit to provide income.

Real Estate

Real Estate is an interesting topic, even if your not going to invest into real estate I would still suggest you join a REIA local to you. Most will provide a great education on houses, how to buy, what to look for, and introduce you to great people to have as contacts.

You could become a landlord, a person that flips houses, whole seller, or even the person that loans money out to those wanting to do such things. Either way, it is a very in-depth arena. This association will also help you understand local laws and different requirements like permits.

Many people write books after they make a fortune in the real estate market, however it is a risk like everything else, you can make it big or you could essentially flop as well. Be careful when dealing with real estate and make sure you have the time to be vested in learning it, and then have time to obtain the data on a deal before pulling the trigger on anything.

Bonds

Bonds are like loans for companies, they promise to pay back the money based on a note at a percentage of interest. The problem is that most bonds markets require an immense amount to buy into. However, for those that are wanting a smaller stage, Street Shares is a great place to start and it is veteran ran, supporting our vets.

As an test bed, $25.00 was put into a bond in January and 6 months later, it has accumulated $0.35 in interest. This may not sound like much, however, it is an account that is planned on being funded more in the future. This still has a higher value than a savings account at this point. The plan on leaving the money here in the account and just helping it grow.

These bonds are great because it helps small business owners, of which 90% are veteran owned, which we should proudly support those that fought wars for us, while making a little profit as well.

The trick to finances is to start early and diversify into many streams of income. Bonds are one way for this process and depending on the bond a stable way of having your money work for you.

CDs

CDs only work if you perform a high amount and perform a strategy called CD ladder. These things have a low interest rate for you to actually gain any money worth while without putting a high amount of money into them.

That being said there is value in this strategy if it is started really early on. However, most places have a minimum amount to put into a CD. So overall unless you save up and start early, there are better areas to put your money to work for you.

Taxes

Work your life, just to pay taxes to a state, to a country, and then on top of that pay sales tax, gratuity tax, communication taxes, fuel tax, and the list goes on. You get hit with Social Security, Medicare, and Federal Income tax. If you do not live in a tax forgiving state then add the State taxation in there as well.

Now that all of that is taken out, go to the store and buy anything, and get hit with a sales tax. Pay your electric bill and look and you find fuel surcharge (tax), environmental charges, public service tax, and several others. So your taxed in just paying your bills, but they do not go to anything except to weigh down the CEO pockets.

Cable is even worse. You have broadcast TV fees, equipment rentals, regulatory recovery fee, Universal Connectivity Charge (socialism at it's best), state and local sales tax, FCC Fee, and the list can go on.

A fee in this concept is nothing more than a tax, without the name, if it wasn't a tax it would be part of the overall bill when they say the service will cost x amount.

Taxation is theft, although we really at this point have no choice but to pay it or go without. Sad thing is the more socialists that spawn, the more taxation will occur. I am still lost on how people can vote for socialist ideology. Nothing is free, it usually comes in the form of taxation.

Now you also have toll roads, with the state saying it is needed to repair roads, however the state taxation you already give is supposed to deal with that, yet greed has even our local and federal governments just forming new ways to tax even more or say a new fee is in place.

The taxation is even worse depending on the state. California and New York has some of the highest taxation going on. People retreat from these states because of the taxation, but then vote to put in the same party that ended up forming those taxes in the other states. It is like they have no intellectual ability to realize it is the political aspect that forms more taxation.

Unfortunately you can not talk about taxation without talking politics, so I will pretty much end this section here, just know there are several things you can do to minimize these taxation and fees.

HSA Accounts

This is a pre-tax medical savings account, one of many ways to cut your taxation, for the time being. It is a good program, and would advise anyone that wants to cut their taxes and still save for any medical payment in the future to participate in these programs.

Conclusion

That will get you generally thinking about different aspects of the financial world. In the next chapter we will start taking on different type of strategies. We will start off with the strategy of a kid and work our way up through life. It should give a great starting point for people, and then of course many people will be in different areas of life looking for the best strategy or a better strategy than what is used, still we advise to review each strategy in the following chapters in order to get more weapons in the financial arena.

Chapter 8

"Starting Strategy"

When we first start life we do not know much about finances, and many do not know how to budget, and for the parents that do not teach their kids budgeting, shame on you, you are horrible parents, of course there is a chance that your parents did not teach you, so your parents are horrible. At some point down the line of family lineage someone knew how to budget.

We can not put the blame solely on the parents, we as individuals have a responsibility to learn as well, and for those that did not learn the importance of budgeting early on, shame on you, don't feel bad though, I was also one of these people. My parents failed me in doing budgets, my education (public schooling) failed me, my grandparents though introduced me on balancing, but never budgeting.

So the failure falls on education, and the three major educators in life, schools, parents and self. The very first thing I hit upon in this book was budgeting because it should be your foundation in the financial world. It should be visited often and not treated as a written in stone object, but a fluid river.

So now that you understand part of it is your fault, and the other part is that you were neglected in the financial knowledge, lets start the beginning of your journey.

You get your first job, you work two weeks and obtain your first paycheck. Now comes the important part, understanding a personal want and a personal need. Need vs want is going to be your biggest question in everything you do. You learned about budgeting during the first few chapters, so it is time to put that to use. Budge for the needs and realize that everything else is a want.

Change your mindset to want and need savings above all else. If your need and want align, then your chances of obtaining it is exponentially increased. Most teenagers will spend money as soon as they get it, but just like what was shown early on, you can do much more and increase your chances of succeeding earlier on in life if you apply budgets and a strong passion to save.

Take some of that money and invest in yourself. Pay for classes, get a book on something you could possibly see yourself doing as a job, or a computer software that you wish to learn and possibly could use during your life on earth. Self investment comes after self payment to savings.

Now say you made it 90 days or so, and now your eligible for some perks of a job. Most notable is the 401k or retirement. Even if your only putting $5.00 per check you should at least contribute something to it. You should also learn how to access the portal and manage your mutual funds. Don't let the company decide for you, manage that thing, and don't be a typical hands off type person. Learn about the system, and check up on it.

Most people are hands off treating the 401k system like it will take care of itself, but that is not correct. If you see the market going down, move it to a safe fund, if you know it is going to go back up, put it in a large cap fund, but early only I would just suggest putting it in the large cap funds, any losses you have can be recouped easily enough, however the more money you get into your account, the better you have to be about thinking about strategy and diversity.

You job is not just what you do for work in this stage it is to learn everything that was not given to you that should have been in the financial world. It is time to strike out and learn about the retirement plans, the saving strategies, the purchasing of large objects such as cars and houses to be prepared for when you do these things. It is time to become independent and show the world you can think on your own and learn on your own.

There is also another concept that those starting out need to understand, and that can be summed up in an old phrase. "Rome was not built in a day." Slow and steady, knowing when you strayed off the path and how to get back on it is just as important as learning the strategies, the concepts, and the terminology. Your not going to become rich over night, but the journey is just as important, the building, the tears, the difficulties, and the joys are just as important.

The next thing to start since you started learning about retirement accounts from work is credit. Starting credit can be a good thing or a bad thing. You should know what type of person you are before you attempt to do this. The oldest brother took me when I was just 16 or 17 and told me a great piece of advice. Don't get a credit card until your in in your mid to late twenties. The reason he gave was because it is easy to spend money you don't have. So my word of warning: "If you spend freely, do what the brother suggested, wait and learn finances before getting a credit card".

I do disagree though, the earlier you work on forming credit and understanding it, the better off you could be over time. So if you are a financially responsible person at this stage I would suggest getting a secure credit card from the bank, in order to start forming credit. It is the easiest way to make sure your responsible with one. Plus it will help you in later strategies.

The first five tasks one has when starting out are: Savings, Self Investment, Retirement, Credit, and Learning. These are your five journeys when you start out, actually many of these journeys will be continual in life. You never do get rid of any of them when you go to the next level of life, if anything it will present more challenges instead of getting easier. Imagine though you did not get the education early on, or the learning and information. You could probably see how you could end up so far in debt you could loose hope.

The only time debt becomes your friend is if you can leverage it, if it is an asset as well as a liability. Try to avoid debt as much as possible that does not fit this scheme. It will be difficult at first, and it will be tricky in determining what fits this criteria.

A house is one of these types of debts, however if you use your car to make money by providing transportation services, then it too would be one of those debts, but normally would not be.

Chapter 9

Snowball Technique

If you have looked into the financial world you probably already heard of this technique. They call it snowball technique. It is a simple idea for small wins quickly, it helps those needing a confidence boost, and to get rid of debt at a decent amount of time.

Snowball is where you pay off one debt, but instead of freeing the payment on said debt, you roll it into the next lowest debt. You are essentially creating a snowball by rolling the money into the next one. Someone had to have some imagination to call it this. But let's focus on the criteria for such a case to do this.

There is a term though I would like to introduce to you before we continue any further, and it is a very important term or idea in the financial world, yet it is hardly ever talked about. Money over Time, MoT is the money either spent over a time frame, or saved over a time frame. You will see where money over time comes into play.

The snowball works like this. You take your smallest debt, and pay it off, adding more to the payment if you can. Once that debt is completed, you take that normal payment and move it to the next lowest debt.

Now while you pay the first lowest balance, you are paying the minimum on all the others. What ever bill you are focused, the others are at the minimum payment.

Now remember debt is to take advantage of people, the longer it takes to pay off the more money the one that offered the loan gets. They eat you with interest. The problem with the concept of snowball is that it does not take into effect interest rates usually. Modify this and take advantage of MoT. Calculate the best option to save the most money over time.

Take for example you have a 12 month loan for 800 at 10% and another for 1000 at 10%. for just 200 dollar difference your MoT is $20.00. If the amount is even 1000 at 9.2% you still save $12.16. Which does not seem like much, but if you don't have much or live from payday to payday, that 12-20 dollars can help you out to make it to the next check.

The point is that even if you read a technique don't be afraid to tear it apart and apply a better logic to it. You don't become wise though just imitation, but by constant revisions, and by constant self thought.

A conversation with a friend was had debating on what to pay first, the house of the vehicle. Calculations of MoT were done and the house would save more money over time vs. the vehicle. Now I could snowball the vehicle, but what if an accident happens and the vehicle is demolished, a new vehicle would need to be purchased and while insurance may cover it, it is usually nothing that comes back to you after the loan is paid off.

The friend kept saying paying the vehicle off first would be better, but if the bills are not impacting me due to a certain strategy, one does not have to rely on snowball, but will take out the highest amount of money first, focusing on the interest rate before the amount. Also the bill on the house is about $100.00 more than the vehicle. So there is the differences in the bills a month.

The point here is that friends will have ideas, and strategies, and even give you advice, however you may have different ideas. It is not wrong to listen to the suggestions, go back crunch numbers and then decide either. However, never listen to people that are not doing better than yourself either. Taking financial advice from those that are not doing right by their finances is a fools bet.

Myself, I don't discard snowball, I like the concept, the problem I have with it from so many sites, is it will not explain the lowest amount, is not always the lowest principle. They do not calculate the differences in the interest rates.

Chapter 10

Leveraging

A phrase actually said when asked about putting finance into one sentence. I love debt, was the response given. This is based off a strategy to kill debt by leveraging an asset that is still a liability. This is done by using the equity in your house to destroy the principle of items.

So how does this concept work? What is needed, and is it better than snowball? The requirements are you need a house with equity, then a Home Equity Line of Credit (HELOC) from your bank, a low interest credit card, and a job that allows you to have more coming in than going out. Most importantly it takes discipline and budgeting. It will become the culmination of all you have learned. Simple process though, and easy to understand.

So to help you understand the flow of the money, please see the below simple graphic.

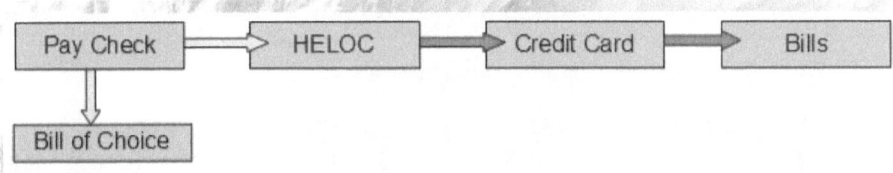

This is how it works, you have a payday, and you put everything to the bill of choice, double points if it is your mortgage. That leaves the bills, and this is where your Credit Card comes in, you pay the bills and lifestyle with the Credit Card. If you have the Credit Card through the bank you will need to call them to find out the date that interest is actually accrued. You pay off the Credit Card about three days before with the HELOC, you can also just do this twice a week when payday comes.

Now all your bills are paid, your Credit Card is paid, and the negative sits in the HELOC. Congratulations on the Credit Card bit, it will help you FICO doing this as well.

For the next 2 or 3 months you follow the other green arrow. You pay the bills with CC, then CC with HELOC, and then HELOC with your entire check. After about 2 or 3 months, your HELOC and CC will be 0. Wash, rinse, repeat.

So let's look under the hood, the car may run, but is it really a good engine? Why buy the car if you just drive it and not inspect it right? So let's look at this. In a matter of a year how much debt do you cut out of your life? Can you get rid of high level bills quickly by the process you currently run? A test of this process was done below:

Car amount: 6,000 roughly 6-7% interest 3 years left

Water Filtration: 12,000 roughly 14% interest, 5 years

Windows: 10,000 roughly, 14% interest, 1 year same as cash

Roof: 11,000 roughly, no interest paid out.

Total debt cleared: 39,000 debt target over 2 years

This is what happens, in this strategy, you take advantage of interest rates, and of crushing the principles. Essentially your freeing up your pay check to destroy large amounts on principle rate. The credit card at 9% or 10% is used for easy access to payments, and the lower HELOC 4% is used to offset the money on the CC. All bills paid and you crushed a bills principle versus the nickle and dime style of normal payments.

The bills include the normal payment of the bill of choice by the way. So essentially you are making a massive entry way into getting rid of the bill quickly. Say a bill is 2000.00 less, the interest collected on the monthly bill will also be less.

This was learned in a book in 1998. Took a while to get the courage up and try it out. Once tried, and completed some bills, it was attempted to revert back to the normal way people live, and it just was not possible to live like that any more.

The discipline comes in because it can be easy to assume you have a bunch of money living on CC, instead of keeping to the budget. Crush principle and you save more money in the long term. How much does this actually cost. Since January 2018, it has only costed 142.30 total in interest rates on the HELOC. Pretty much pennies compared to the saving on interests or the getting out from under bills.

Amount	Balance
-11 57	-11 57
-13 35	-24 92
-9 92	-34 84
-11 00	-45 84
-11 66	-57 50
-15 10	-72 60
-8 01	-80 61
-12 72	-93 33
-4 41	-97 74
-4 17	-101 91
-1 75	-103 66
-4 89	-108 55
-3 34	-111 89
-0 48	-112 37
-8 42	-120 79
-5 83	-126 62
-15 68	-142 30

This process was developed in order to pay off a house quickly and kill the interest collected by the mortgage companies. Most mortgage companies and banks in the United States does not teach this strategy because it would cut into the profits by the interest rate. However they are not against a person using it either. If a person pays back their loan quickly they do not have to worry about a default and can use that money to fund another loan.

The trick on any bill you apply this to is to make sure there is no penalty for paying early, and if there is, question ever doing business with that company again. Anyone that wants to penalize another for paying off their debt quickly is a very shady business partner.

It is a very cool strategy to work with, and allows the ability to crush any debt your have, and can fully be utilized with snowball, so yes it is better than snowballing, but in a different way since it can incorporate the technique as well.

This was introduced to a couple of people, however one lost the ability to, due to the financial habits they had, and the other just has not followed through on getting the HELOC aspect completed. So how do you start all of it?

Good news is you already have the house, and the job or paycheck, which means you probably have a credit card already as well. Just means you need the HELOC and strategy your going to do. This of course takes into account your adept at budgeting as well.

Go to your bank and tell them you want to setup an account to help them make money so it helps you make money. When they look at you weird and they will, you look at them and say you wish to open a HELOC so you can utilize your entire paycheck for the ability to crush principles on debts.

This will spark the interest of the banker and as they process the HELOC, they will ask how you plan on doing this. Once you tell them the strategy they will look impressed and say it is smart. Of course they already knew of the process before you tell them. It is just they are impressed you found out about it. Remember this is a highly guarded secret the banks do not tell anyone.

There are complete books written on this strategy; however this is the strategy without the fluff. It really is that simple, moving money between accounts is all your really doing in order to kill principle, but you do live in a negative until the HELOC is zeroed out. Hence the reason, I love debt is the subtitle of this chapter.

Chapter 11

Passive Stream

If you look up passive income in a google or bing search, you will come across many solutions, but rarely something that is really passive. This book that is being written can not even be considered passive, in the eyes of the author. For one it did not take minimum effort to wright this for everyone. While it may generate revenue and I thank those that buy this book, it still took much to write it.

So if a book is not considered passive, what can be considered passive? Let's destroy the concept of passive real quick by looking at a list of what others consider passive.

Real Estate no matter how you look at it is not as passive as one thinks. The only way real estate is passive is if do a REIT or crowd funded solution. The traditional aspect of flipping houses or renting houses are not as passive as one thinks.

First you need to find the house, then find contractors to fix it up, or find renters, and then find contractors to fix things as they break, or fix it yourself. Either way it is not so passive in this aspect. I consider little to no effort passive. Truly passive income is the essential ideology of having your money work for you.

Investing is another item these sites all state. However, most people already do this in their 401k. Investing that they talk about is stocks , and usually refer you to apps on a phone that has a high rate, compared to places like eTrade, before following these trends, investigate what you will pay before you get sucked into them.

Now if your into stocks through a normal venue, then it takes some effort, it takes a careful eye, even if your a fundamental investor or dividend investor. It still takes some effort on your part to keep things from going belly up as it were. We do not want this raft we are on tipping over because we had to perform something and didn't, or performed something we didn't have to do.

Depending on skill, they consider peer to peer lending part of investing, which actually everything you do that has a potential of making money back or making more money is an investment. Peer to peer lending can be fully automated, and while even stock trading can as well, the options of APIs in the lending seem a little easier to grasp than those on things like eTrade and stock platforms.

For example with some python language skills one can program a robot that sits on the desktop. The Robot queries the account and waits for a threshold to hit. Once that threshold hits, it then begins the process of buying a loan based of logic and configuration items you dictate to it. This is essentially a true formula of getting to complete passive income.

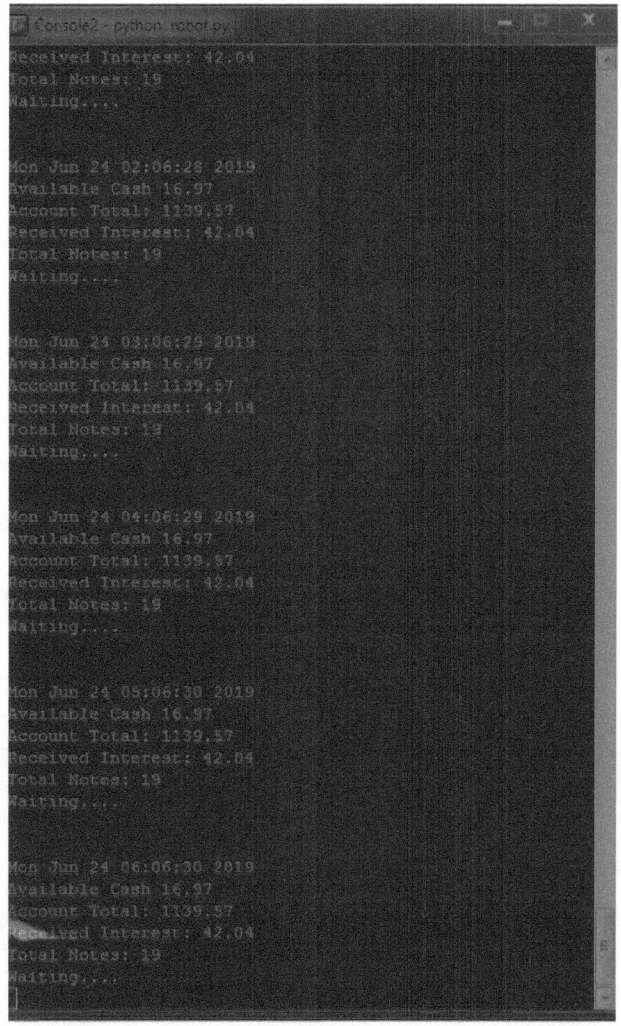

Starting a blog or buying a blog, which unfortunately is not passive. It takes time it takes a good effort to upkeep a blog, keep your audience coming back and either donating or obtaining cash via advertisements. Not something to really be considered passive.

Drop shipping could be considered passive after you setup the website and set prices, however it really does take a little effort after the fact of tracking prices and doing a price war if that is what is needed to keep clients coming back, the other issue with this is that the market space is so saturated it is hard to get into anymore. Plus there is Amazon giant to contend with.

Writing a book, like this one, or on a different subject, can become passive. The font end work though is massive, and time consuming. Writing a book can be very time consuming. Then publishing, which is easier with electronic publishing, and then pricing. It can become a very intense project to work upon.

The definition of passive equates to all these, but to be fully passive, the project has to enter a completion state, and then to a point where it makes money without you doing anything. It is just trickling money in without intervention.

As a network analyst/ engineer, I did not need to learn a programming language but did just as a hobby. That hobby allowed me to program a fully automated way in Lending Club to get to a passive income. This goes back to what I said about self investments, if you gain knowledge you can do many things in life.

Another hobby is the study money, listen to finance podcasts, and teach others what is learned. It is a great way to help others out and get them on the path of looking for Financial Independence or financial stability at the very least.

One could write a course and put on a site and sell. Suggest staying away from those though, a book you can reference the rest of life is more valuable than a course you access once.

Automation is the bane of workers, however if your one of the ones putting together the automation, then it is not so much a bane, but an opportunity. Instead of having an issue with how a business is going to go, be one of the ones that drive it, engineer it, and maintains it. Change the view you have and make an opportunity instead of a disaster.

Study psychology, theology, philosophy, and many other aspects of the human mind. That way you can read and determine how a person is going to act or react, then you can maneuver the environment to your benefit instead of your challenge.

www.ingramcontent.com/pod-product-compliance
Lightning Source LLC
Chambersburg PA
CBHW030952240526
45463CB00016B/2510